"Dreamtime Gecko"
Artist: Vanessa Wells

VOICE. TREATY. TRUTH.
ULURU STATEMENT FROM THE HEART

We, gathered at the 2017 National Constitutional Convention, coming from all points of the southern sky, make this statement from the heart:

Our Aboriginal and Torres Strait Islander tribes were the first sovereign Nations of the Australian continent and its adjacent islands, and possessed it under our own laws and customs. This our ancestors did, according to the reckoning of our culture, from the Creation, according to the common law from 'time immemorial', and according to science more than 60,000 years ago.

This sovereignty is a spiritual notion: the ancestral tie between the land, or 'mother nature', and the Aboriginal and Torres Strait Islander peoples who were born therefrom, remain attached thereto, and must one day return thither to be united with our ancestors. This link is the basis of the ownership of the soil, or better, of sovereignty. It has never been ceded or extinguished, and co-exists with the sovereignty of the Crown.

How could it be otherwise? That peoples possessed a land for sixty millennia and this sacred link disappears from world history in merely the last two hundred years?

With substantive constitutional change and structural reform, we believe this ancient sovereignty can shine through as a fuller expression of Australia's nationhood.

Proportionally, we are the most incarcerated people on the planet. We are not an innately criminal people. Our children are aliened from their families at unprecedented rates. This cannot be because we have no love for them. And our youth languish in detention in obscene numbers. They should be our hope for the future.

These dimensions of our crisis tell plainly the structural nature of our problem. This is the torment of our powerlessness.

We seek constitutional reforms to empower our people and take a rightful place in our own country. When we have power over our destiny our children will flourish. They will walk in two worlds and their culture will be a gift to their country.

We call for the establishment of a First Nations Voice enshrined in the Constitution.

Makarrata is the culmination of our agenda: the coming together after a struggle. It captures our aspirations for a fair and truthful relationship with the people of Australia and a better future for our children based on justice and self-determination.

We seek a Makarrata Commission to supervise a process of agreement-making between governments and First Nations and truth-telling about our history.

In 1967 we were counted, in 2017 we seek to be heard. We leave base camp and start our trek across this vast country. We invite you to walk with us in a movement of the Australian people for a better future.

This consensus followed a ground-breaking process First Nations from across Australia through 12 deliberative dialogues. Joining each dialogue were a representative sample of approximately 100 Indigenous people drawn from local traditional owners, Indigenous community-based organisations and Indigenous leaders. These regional dialogues selected their own representatives to attend the First Nations Constitutional Convention at Uluru. At the Convention, and by an overwhelming consensus, more than 250 delegates adopted the Uluru Statement.

A First Nations Voice to Parliament.
The voice to parliament would be a representative body giving Aboriginal and Torres Strait Islanders a say in law and policy affecting them. Enshrined in the constitution, it would become an institution of lasting significance for First Nations and all Australians.

You know what it's like to be frustrated, alone and full of anger in a moment as life happens to you. It's that feeling of not having control over any of it is the hardest to get through.

I'd like to share something with you very personal to me. Would that be ok? Growing up in school, I was bullied, rejected and feeling less than normal because I grew up very overweight.

Kids never hesitated to let me know just how different I was from them. Not feeling people saw me for the loving, sweet person I was, but odd and apart from anyone around me. I was a tortured soul, just trying to fit in.

Today, I know there is a difference in the people who see you and who you see. Not for our differences but for what brings us together.

Having compassion for everyone and moving through this little blue planet knowing we are not our struggles but an opportunity to see differently.

This is a book of poems for those of you who are going through some things.

What a great compilation of poems about the struggles of life of a tortured mind then know there is much solice that comes through.

It's a work written that appeals to the human spirit. Knowing you are not alone.

Thank you "The Don" for sharing these works with the world. And thank you all for supporting this great writer and my friend.

Cheers!

Katrina Gorman
October, 2020

"The Don"
Artist: Katrina Gorman
www.Katrinagormandesigns.com

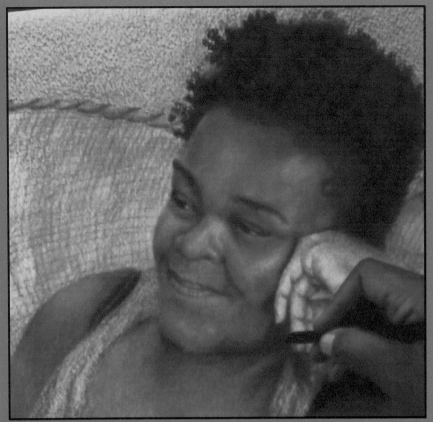

Katrina Gorman 2020

"Self-portrait"
Artist: Katrina Gorman
www.katrinagormandesigns.com

Contents

Contents

Contents

You Just Like Him Because He's Good in Bed!

(Ti Piace Solo Perché è Bravo a Letto!)

You just like him 'cause he's good in bed.
That's what you said.
"*He's fucking amazing*"!
That's what you said.

I fell to the floor.
I got down on my knees.
I begged you, "please".
"*Please, please, please*"!

There's nothing more I can do.
There's nothing more I can say.
I just have put my tail between my legs.
I just have to walk away.

When someone tells you that.
You know that you have no hope.
How can you compete?
You're not even in the race.

I'm pretty good too.
Just give me a chance.
I have a few skills up my sleeve.
How good can he be?

Maybe, I too am good in bed?
How do you know if you haven't tried?
Try me out.
Take me for a test drive.
Maybe you could like me too, 'cause I'm good bed.

You just like him 'cause he's good in bed.
That's what you said.

"The Don"
11.09.2020

Inside is Outside

(Dentro è Fuori)

What is inside is outside.
What is outside is inside.
The two are inexplicably linked.
They are one & the same.
There is no separation.
There is no division.
The unity if the whole.

The external is the internal.
The internal is the time external.
They are one & the same.
The interconnection of things.
The inter-relation is dynamic.
The two are one & the same.

The external environment is your internal environment.
Your internal environment is your external environment.
The two are one & the same.
There is no separation.
There is no division.
The two are intimately entwined.

Like two dancers on the dance floor.
Two Lo♥ers, entwined in each others arms.
Two people making Lo♥e.
The two are one.
There two become one.
There is no separation.

This is the nature of things.
This is the relationship of Life.
This is the relationship of the Universe.
This is the "*Cosmic*" dance.
This is what binds us.
This is what connects us.
This is the "*Mobius Loop*".

We are not separate entities.
We are not individual atoms.
We are not alone.
We are not disconnected.
We are not untethered.
We are not unbound.
We are not unlinked.

We are "*one*" Being.
We are "*one*" Whole.
We are "*one*" Consciousness.
We are "*one*" Thought.
We are "*one*".

"The Don"
11.09.2020

Born Naked

(Nato Nudo)

We are all born without clothes.
We are all born with no clothes on.
We are all born naked.

Why do we wear clothes?
Why do we cover or bodies?
We are all born naked.

Is just to keep warm?
Is just protect ourselves?
We are all born naked.

Or is it something more sinister?
Are we ashamed of our nakedness?
We are all born naked.

Are we embarrassed with our bodies?
Told to cover up.
We are all born naked.

Told that it's wrong to be naked.
Told that it's bad not to wear clothes.
But we are all born naked.

We are told of "Social Decency".
We are told that we must cover up.
But we are all born naked.

It is "Indecent" to go naked in public.
It is a crime not to wear clothes outside.
But we are all born naked.

Children would be harmed.
They would be traumatised, they say.
But we are all born naked.

What is so wrong being naked?
What is so wrong going without clothes?
But we are all born naked.

Who said that this is wrong?
Who said that this is bad?
We are all born naked.

When did this "fake" morality start?
When did it become "indecent"?
We are all born naked.

There is nothing wrong with being naked.
There is nothing to be embarrassed about.
There is nothing to be ashamed over.
We are all born naked.

Our naked bodies are beautiful.
Our naked bodies are a natural thing.
Our naked bodies are a part of Nature.
We are all born naked.

Embrace being naked.
Let it all hang out.
Don't be ashamed of getting naked.
Don't be embarrassed with your naked self.
"Take it all off", I say.
It's a better way to live.
Society would have less social hang ups.
It would be a much better place than today.
Because we are all born naked.

Born Naked

"The Don"
11.09.2020

An Ideal World

(Un Mondo Ideale)

No *wars*.
No *violence*.
No *exploitation*.
No *discrimination*.
No *abuse*.
No *inequality*.
No *poverty*.
No *hunger*.
No *racism*.
No *hatred*.
No *killing*.
No *borders*.
No *destruction of the environment*.

Is it even *possible*?
Is it just a *dream*?
Is it just an *illusion*?
Is it just a *delusion*?
Is it just a *fanciful desire*?
Is it just an *unobtainable ideal*?

Can it ever even exist?

An Ideal World!

"The Don"
12.09.2020

Not Allowed to Wear a Cap!

(Non è Consentito Indossare un Berretto)

I was sitting in one of my local pubs.
I was watching the footy.
The Roosters versus The Knights.
I was drinking a scooter of beer.
A low cab beer in fact.
I'm on a diet.
Minding my own business.
When the barman came over & told me.
"Sir, you'll have to take your cap off!"
Yes, I was wearing my cap.
"What?", I replied.
"You can't wear a cap inside the pub!"
he stated.
"You've got to be joking!" I retorted in disbelief.
"It's something to do with gaming & facial recognition" he tried to explain.
Although I'm sure he really had no real idea why himself.
So, with incredulity, I took my cap off.

What the hell is going on?
I had already had been asked & for my photo ID on entry.
Had asked for a contact number.
And had my temperature taken.
I'm surprised they didn't ask for the length of my cock!
What the FUCK!
Are we living in a police state or what?
Fascism reigns supreme!

Although, fortunately, it was a great game of footy!

"The Don"
12.09.2020

Needy

(Bisognoso)

Don't be needy.
Don't be greedy.
Don't be seedy.
Don't be touchy feely.

You're a pussy.
You're too easy.
You're so predictable.
You're too needy.

That won't get you anywhere.
That won't get you what you want.
That won't get you what you need.
You're too needy.

Play it cool.
Play it aloof.
Play it again, Sam.
But don't be needy.

Show that you don't care.
Show that you're not interested.
Show no emotions.
But don't be needy.

Be detached.
Be cold.
Be uninterested.
But don't be needy.

Better to be vague.
Better to be remote.
Better to be distant.
But don't be needy.

"The Don"
13.09.2020

You Are Beautiful!

(Sei Bella)

We take people for granted.
We assume that they'll always be there.
We don't tell them often enough that they are beautiful.
We don't tell them often enough that we Lo♥e them.
So, I'll say it now.
I'll say it in a poem.
You are BEAUTIFUL!

My selfish needs get in the way.
My selfish desires make me blind.
My selfish needs divert me
My selfish appetites consume me.
My selfish passions devour me.
My selfish He♥rt controls me.

I don't see what is right in front of me.
I don't see my nose on my face.
I don't see your amazing beauty.
I don't see it when it's staring me in my face.
I don't see it because I am blind.
I don't see it because I am not looking.
I don't see you because I don't see.
I don't see you because I am selfish.

I don't tell you enough.
So, I'll tell it to you now.
I'll tell it in a poem.
You are BEAUTIFUL!

You are most beautiful person in the whole World.
You are most beautiful person in the whole Universe.
You are most beautiful person in the whole Multiverse.
You are most beautiful person in the whole Cosmos.

I don't tell you enough.
So, I'll tell it to you now.
I'll tell it in a poem.
You are BEAUTIFUL!

"The Don"
14.09.2020

Do Not Seek the Treasure!

(Non Cercare il Tesoro!)

Do not seek the "*Pot of Gold*".
Do not seek the "*End of the Rainbow*".
Do not seek the "*Holy Grail*".
Do not seek the "*Library of Alexandria*".
Do not seek the "*Aztec Civilisation*".
Do not seek the "*Treasures of The Mayan Civilisation*".
Do not seek the "*Lost Land of Atlantis*".
Do not seek the "*Treasures of the Ancient Mesopotamian World*".
Do not seek the "*Treasure of the Sierra Madre*".
Do not seek the "*Treasures of Tutankhamun*".
Do not seek the "*Treasures of the Vatican*".
Do not seek the "*Iron Throne*".
Do not seek the "*Golden Orb & Sceptre*".
Do not seek the "*Crown Jewels*".
Do not seek the "*Pleasure Dome*".

Do not seek "*Nirvana*".
Do not seek "*El Dorado*".
Do not seek "*Shangri-la*".
Do not seek "*Ali Baba's Cave*".
Do not seek "*King Solomon's Mines*".
Do not seek "*Nefertiti's Treasure*".
Do not seek "*King Arthur's Sword*".
Do not seek "*Thor's Hammer*".
Do not seek "*Poseidon's Trident*".
Do not seek "*Jesus Christ's Crown of Thorns*".
Do not seek the "*Shroud of Turin*".
Do not seek the "*Pearly Gates*".
Do not seek "*Heaven*".

Do NOT seek the TREASURE!

"The Don"
14.09.2020

Blood on Your Hands

(Sangue sulle tue Mani)

I have blood on my hands.
You have blood on your hands
We all have blood on our hands.
Society has blood on its hands.
Capitalism has blood on its hands.
Communism has blood on its hands.
Fascism has blood on its hand.
Politicians have blood on their hands.
The rich have blood on their hands.
The aristocracy have blood on their hands.
The Monarchy has blood on its hands.
Priests have blood on their hands.
The Church has blood on its hands.
Religions have blood on their hands.
The military industrial complex has blood on its hands.
The USA has blood on its hands.
Great Britain has blood on its hands.
France has blood on its hands.
Spain has blood on its hands.
Germany has blood on its hands.
Russia has blood on its hand.
ISIS has blood on its hands.
The Ayatollah has blood on his hands.
"*The White Man*" has blood on its hands.
God has blood on his hands.
The Devil has blood on his hands.

The Poor do not have blood on their hands.
The exploited do not have blood on their hands.
The discriminated do not have blood on their hands.
First Nations Peoples do not have blood on their hands.
Indigenous Peoples do not have blood on their hands.
Women do not have blood on their hands.
Children do not have blood on their hands.

Do you have blood on your hands?

"The Don"
14.09.2020

Acceptance

(Accettazione)

Resignation to the situation.
Facing the inevitable.
Realising where you stand.
Acknowledgement of the facts.
Acceptance of "what is".
Seeing "what is not".
Finding "Reality".
Accepting disappointment.
Becoming "grounded".
Overcoming the feeling of being "let down".
Looking forward.
Moving on.
Not standing still.
Weight off one's shoulders.
Feeling lighter.
Although feeling empty.
Nothing you can do.
That's life.
It is what it is.
Get over it.

Accept rejection.
Accept sadness.
Accept failure.
Accept emptiness.
Accept loneliness.
Accept sorrow.
Accept resignation.
Accept loss.
Accept tears.
Accept a broken He♥rt.
Accept unrequited Lo♥e.
Accept acceptance.

"The Don"
15.09.2020

There Once Was

(C'era Una Volta)

There once was
a singer who could not sing.
There once was
an illiterate that was a philosopher.
There once was
a pauper that died wealthy.
There once was
a short man that lived a tall life.
There once was
a poet that couldn't see.
There once was
musician that couldn't hear.
There once was
a Lo♥er that didn't have any Lo♥e.
There once was
a living man who really was dead.
There once was
an economist that knew nothing about money.
There once was
a priest that didn't believe in God.
There once was
a politician that was honest.
There once was
a judicial system that was just.
There once was
a government that worked for the people.
There once was
a society where everyone was equal.
There once was
a system that wasn't corrupt.
There once was
a young boy that had old thoughts.
There once was
an old man who thought he was young.
There once was
an old man that didn't want to die.
There once was
a baby that didn't want to be born.
There once was a chemical engineer that became a poet.

"The Don"
15.09.2020

Do not

Do not *touch me*.
Do not *feel me*.
Do not *be so "touchy feely"*.
Do not *put your hands on me*.
Do not *soothe me*.
Do not *hug me*.
Do not *heal me*.
Do not *get too close to me*.
Do not *put your arms around me*.
Do not *kiss me*.
Do not *lick me*.
Do not *suck me*.
Do not *bite me*.
Do not *poke me*.
Do not *prod me*.
Do not *stroke me*.
Do not *hold me*.
Do not *look at me*.
Do not *feed me*.
Do not *seed me*.
Do not *adore me*.
Do not *worship me*.
Do not *praise me*.
Do not *follow me*.
Do not *stalk me*.
Do not *seek me*.
Do not *find me*.
Do not *lose me*.
Do not *free me*.
Do not *eat me*.
Do not *Lo♥e me*.
Do not *HATE me*.

"The Don"
15.09.2020

Is Orange Still Orange?

(Orange è Ancora Arancione?)

Is "The Lady in Red" still wearing red?
Is "Purple Rain" still purple?
Is "Blue Velvet" still blue?
Is the "Yellow Brick Road" still yellow?
Is "The Wind That Cries Mary" still crying?
Is "Proud Mary" still proud?
Is "Murder Most Foul" still foul?
Is the "Cowgirl in the Sand" still in the sand?
Is "Copperhead Road" still a road?
Is "Highway 61" still a highway?
Is "Heartbreak Hotel" still a hotel?
Is "Hotel California" still in California?
Is the "Midnight Rambler" still rambling?
Is "The Tallest Man on Earth" still the tallest?
Is the "Idiot Wind" still an idiot?
Is "Silence is Golden" still golden?
Is "The Sound of Silence" still silent?
Is "The Lady from The Red River Shore" still at Red River?
Is "The Ferryman" still a ferryman?
Is the "Highway to Hell" still going to Hell?
Is "It's a Long Way to the Top" still a long way?
Is "Symphony for the Devil" still a symphony?
Is "Thick as a Brick" still thick?
Is "In A Gadda Da Vida" still in Vida?
Is "Iron Butterfly" still a butterfly?
Is the "Stairway to Heaven" still going to Heaven?
Is "Green River" still green?
Is "Morrison Hotel" still a hotel?
Is "Roadhouse Blues" still a roadhouse?
Is "Funeral for a Friend" still a friend?
Is "Pavlov's Dog" still Pavlov's?
Is "Thor's Hammer" still Thor's?
Is "Hard Rock" still hard?
Is "Rock"n'Roll" still rocking'n'rolling?

Is "Doc Watson" still a Doc?
Is "Blind Willie McTell" still blind?
Is "Summertime Blues" still summertime?
Is "The Weeping Song" still weeping?
Is "The Stranger Song" still a stranger?
Is "The Tower Song" still a song?
Is "Red Right Hand" still red?
Is "One More Cup of Coffee for the Road" still only one cup of coffee?
Is "10 minutes to Midnight" still 10 minutes?
Is "Paint it Black" still black?
Is "The Song of Joy" still joyful?
Is "The Girl from Ipanema" still in Ipanema?
Is the "Great Southern Land" still great?
Is "Monkey Man" still a monkey?
Is "The Season of the Witch" still the season of the witch?
Is "The Lost Civilisation of Atlantis" still lost?
Is "Lo♥e is Just a 4 Letter Word" still just a 4 Letter word?

Are "Deep Purple" still deep?
Are "The Moody Blues" still moody?
Are "The Rolling Stones" still rolling?
Are "The Guess Who" still guessing?
Are "The Monkeys" still monkeys?
Are "The Searchers" still searching?
Are "The Police" still police?
Are "The Honey Drippers" still dripping honey?
Are "The Buffalo Boys" still boys?
Are "Girls Just Wanna Have Fun" still just wanting to have fun?
Are "The Zombies" still zombies?
Are "The Stranglers" still strangling?
Are "Aesop's Fables" still fables?
Are "The Red Hot Chilli Peppers" still hot?
Are "Willie & the Poor Boys" still poor?
Are "The Boys are Back in Town" still in town?

Is Orange still Orange?

"The Don"
15.09.2020

Family

(Famiglia)

Brother, oh brother.
Sister, oh sister.
Mother, oh mother.
Father, oh father.
Daughter, oh daughter.
Son, oh son.
Friend, oh friend.
Lo♥er, oh Lo♥er.
Earth, oh Earth.
Moon, oh Moon.
Venus, oh Venus.
Mars, oh Mars.
Sun, oh Sun
Stars, oh stars.
Galaxy, oh galaxy.
Universe, oh Universe.
Cosmos, oh Cosmos.
Life, oh Life.
Death, oh Death
He♥rt, oh He♥rt.
Soul, oh Soul.
Human, oh Human.

"The Don"
16.09.2020

Earth is in Heart

(La Terra è nel Cuore)

Art is in Heart.
Art is in Hearth.
Art is in Artery.
Art is in Smart.
Art is in Part.
Art is in Apart.
Art is in Party.
Art is in Fart.
Art is in Chart.
Art is in Tart.
Art is in Start.
Art is in Cart.
Art is in Cartoon.
Art is in Depart.
Art is in Barter.
Art is in Artifice.
Art is in Artisan.
Art is in Artistic.
Art is in Artificial.
Art is in Artificiality.
Art is in Artifice.
Art is in Articulate.
Art is in Articulation.
Art is in Participate.
Art is in Participation.
Art is in Particle
Art is in Particular
Art is in Particularity.
Art is in SingulaARiTy
Art is in Compartment.
Art is in Department.
Art is in CReATe.
Art is in CrReATive.
Art is in CReATivity.
Art is in CReATion.

"The Don"
16.09.2020

Puppet on a String

(Burattino Su Una Corda)

Pull me this way.
Pull me that way.
Bend me here.
Bend me there.

Tell me what to do.
Tell me where to go.
Tell me what to say.
Tell me what to think.
Tell me what to feel.

You are in control of me.
You are in the driver's chair.
You are in the cockpit.
You are in my mind.

You are the boss of me.
You are my mind.
You have total control.
You pull the strings.

I have no thoughts of my own.
I have no mind of my own
I have no actions of my own.
I have no decisions of my own.
I have no feelings of my own.

I am just a "Puppet on a String".

"I wonder if one day that,
You'll say that, you care
If you say you love me madly,
I'll gladly, be there
Like a puppet on a string."

"Love is just like a merry-go-round
With all the fun of the fair
One day I'm feeling down on the ground
Then I'm up in the air
Are you leading me on?
Tomorrow will you be gone?

I wonder if one day that,
You'll say that, you care
If you love me madly,
I'll gladly, be there
Like a puppet on a string.

I may win on the roundabout
Then I'll lose on the swings
In or out, there is never a doubt
Just who's pulling the strings
I'm all tied up to you
But where's it leading me to?

I wonder if one day that,
You'll say that, you care
If you say you love me madly,
I'll gladly, be there
Like a puppet on a string,

I wonder if one day that,
You'll say that, you care
If you say you love me madly,
I'll gladly, be there
Like a puppet on a string

Like a puppet on a, string."

"Writer/s: Bill Martin, Phil Coulter, Performed by: Sandy Shaw"

Do Not Pursue

(Non Perseguire)

Do not chase.
Do not follow.
Do not run after.
Do not stalk.
Do not fantasise.
Do not dream about.
Do not Desire.
Do not Want.
Do not fetishise.
Do not idolise.
Do not worship.
Do not become attached.
Do not become obsessed.
Do not become possessed.
Do not become enchained.
Do not become infatuated.
Do not crawl.
Do not beg.
Do not grovel.
Do not be easy.
Do not be a "Pussy".
Do not go crazy.

Do not fall in Lo♥e.
And if you do.
Do not pursue!

"The Don"
17.09.2020

Renegade

(Rinnegata)

You live on the *edge*.
You're nobody's *fool*.
No one tells you what to *do*.
You break all the *rules*.
You don't do what you're *told*.
You live by your own *rules*.
Nobody's gonna fuck with you.
You're a renegade.

You live by your own *rules*.
You live your life your own *way*.
You do what you wanna do.
You do it when you wanna do it.
You do it with whomever you wanna do it with.
You do it wherever you wanna do.
You're a renegade.

Life's too short to be messed around.
You have no time for fools to tell you what to do.
No fucking idiots gonna push you around.
You're not gonna be pushed around for their entertainment.
You're not their little plaything.
You're a renegade.

You ride your own *horse*.
You drive your own *car*.
You walk your own *path*.
You follow your own *road*.
Your destiny is yours & yours alone.
Ain't no fuckwit gonna fuck you around.
You're a renegade.

You're your own *boss*.
You're your own *chief*.
You're you own *leader*.
You're you own *voice*.
You're your own *gun*.
In fact, you're *"Janie's got a gun"*.
You're a *"Rebel with a cause"*.
You're a *"Real Wild Child"*.
You're a fucking renegade.

"The Don"
17.09.2020

Leave It to Fate

(Lascialo al Destino)

Fate seems to know what to do.
Fate has all the answers.
Fate solves all your problems.
Fate calms all your worries.
Fate puts you on the "Right" path.
Fate shows you the way.
Fate doesn't hesitate.
Fate doesn't procrastinate.
Fate has no doubts.
Fate doesn't "second guess" itself.
Fate just has one direction.
Fate always moves FORWARD.
Fate doesn't take any detours.
Fate doesn't take a break.
Fate doesn't rest.
Fate doesn't slow down.
Fate doesn't stop.
Fate doesn't stop for anyone.
Fate just keeps on moving on.
Fate just "keeps on keeping on".
Fate will not let you down.
Fate is always by your side.
Fate is one step ahead of you.
Fate is your friend.
Fate is your only friend.
Fate is always there.
Fate has the keys.
Fate unlocks the doors.
Fate is trustworthy.
Fate is dependable.
Fate is your FUTURE.
Fate is who you are.
Fate is whom you are meant to be.
Fate is who you will be.
Fate is YOU.

So, don't worry about it.
Don't worry about anything.
Just leave it to *Fate*.
Fate will NEVER let you down.
And everything will work out.
Everything will work out just fine.
The way it's meant to work.
The way it's meant to be.
Because *Fate* has done its job.

Leave it to *Fate*.

"The Don"
18.09.2020

I Wish

(Spero Che)

I wish for money.
I wish for for happiness.
I wish for for a long life.
I wish for for good health.
I wish for a good job.
I wish to travel.
I wish to see the world.
I wish for the end to violence.
I wish for the end to wars.
I wish for World Peace.
I wish for equality.
I wish for the end of exploitation.
I wish for the end of discrimination.
I wish for end of racism.
I wish for friendships.
I wish for a long life.
I wish for Moon base.
I wish for Humans to colonise Mars.
I wish for "Honest" politicians.
I wish for politicians to keep their promises.
I wish for governments to tackle climate change.
I wish for the demise of Capitalism.
I wish for the equal distribution of wealth.
I wish for super powers.

I wish for sex.
I wish for you.
I wish for Lo♥e.

I wish I could make you Lo♥e me.
I wish!
I wish!
I wish!
I wish in vain.

"The Don"
18.09.2020

Tell Me Why?

(Dimmi Perchè)

Tell me why is it so hard to be at peace?
Tell me why is it so hard to be free?
Tell me why is it so hard to be happy?
Tell me why is it so hard to be positive?
Tell me why is it so hard to be optimistic?
Tell me why is it so hard to be respectful?
Tell me why is it so hard to be compassionate?
Tell me why is it so hard to be kind?
Tell me why is it so hard to be caring?
Tell me why is it so hard to be friendly?
Tell me why is it so hard to be honest?
Tell me why is it so hard to be loyal?
Tell me why is it so hard to be intelligent?
Tell me why is it so hard to be fair?
Tell me why is it so hard to be egalitarian?
Tell me why is it so hard to be poetic?
Tell me why is it so hard to be creative?
Tell me why is it so hard to be sane?
Tell me why is it so hard to be moral?
Tell me why is it so hard to be principled?
Tell me why is it so hard to be an innocent?
Tell me why is it so hard to be a child?
Tell me why is it so hard to be cosmic?
Tell me why is it so hard to be spiritual?
Tell me why is it so hard to be open minded?
Tell me why is it so hard to be thoughtful?
Tell me why is it so hard to be nurturing?
Tell me why is it so hard to be an example?
Tell me why is it so hard to be stress free?
Tell me why is it so hard to be awesome?
Tell me why is it so hard to be a hero?
Tell me why is it so hard to be Lo♥ed?
Tell me why is it so hard to be Lo♥ing?
Tell me why is it so hard to be alive?
Tell me why is it so hard to be Humane?
Tell me why is it so hard to be Human?
Tell me why is it so?
Tell me why?

"The Don"
19.09.2020

Codes

(Codici)

Words are a code.
Language is a code.
Mathematics is a code.
Chemistry is a code.
Physics is a code.
Science is a code.
Religion is a code.
Humour is a code.
Emotions are a code.
Logarithms are a code.
Communication is a code.
Politics is a code.
Society is a code.
Friendship is a code.
The Universe is a code.
The Cosmos is a code.
Hate is a code.
Sex is a code.
Making Love is a code.
Love is a code.
Humanity is a code.
You are a code.
I am a code.
We all are a code.
Everything is a code.

You need a code to unlock a code.
Can you unlock the Code?
Do you have the Code?

"The Don"
19 09.2020

Respect

(Rispetto)

Show me some time Respect.
Show me some Dignity.
Treat me with Lo♥e.
Treat me with kindness.
Don't be mean or unpleasant.
There is no need for such behaviour.

Put your attitude back in your pocket.
Leave it on the shelf.
There ain't no need for disrespect.
There ain't no place for bad treatment.
Show me some maturity.
Show me some intelligence.
You are way better than that my friend.
Show me some respect that all I'm sayin'.

Life is too short for such shit.
Let's not waste it on such trivial matters.
There's much more at stake here.
There are much more important matters to attend too.

Society is in disarray.
The System is breaking down.
Governments have no solutions.
In fact, they are committing the crimes.
The Planet is burning up.
We are destroying everything I'm sigh.
So, let's focus on the "Bigger picture".
Let's get the "basics" right.

It starts with respect my friend.
Respect is the answer.
Respect is all we need to do.
Respect EVERYTHING.
It's as easy as that.
RESPECT!

"The Don"
19.09.2020

It's the End

(È la Fine)

I accept defeat.
The other guy won.
I'm throwing in the towel.
I know when I've been defeat.
I know when the game is over.
I know when the ref has blown his whistle.
It's all over.

I gave it my best shot.
I gave it my all.
I tried my best.
I came short.
I'll walk away.
I'll bid you adieu.
I'll say my goodbyes.
I'll close the curtain.

There's nothing else for me to say.
There's nothing else for me to do.
I'll just drown my sorrows in a scotch & coke.
I'll just drown my sorrows in another gin & tonic.

I gave you all I had.
I gave you my He❤rt.
I gave you my Lo❤e.
But obviously, it was not enough.
The only thing that's left for me to say.
Is, "Have a good life."
"Goodbye."
"Maybe we'll meet again someday."
"Under different circumstances."

"The Don"
19.09.2020

Life is a War of Attrition!

(La Vita è una Guerra di Logoramento!)

Life is a battle that's for sure.
I'll wear your down.
It'll drop you to the floor.
It seems no matter how hard you try.
You can never get on top of it.
Sooner or later you're gonna feel the weight of it.

Like the "water drop torture".
Innocuous at first but over time.
Drop by drop it'll break you down.
Before you know it your flat on your back.
Life has done its job.
You've fought "the good fight".
You've given your "best shot".
You've tried you hardest.
You have it your all.
You put your He♥rt & Soul into it.
And this is where it's got you.
It's not your fault.

The game was rigged from the start.
You weren't to know.
You weren't given the rules.
You were told that this was a *"set up"*.
You never STOOD a chance.
You could NEVER win.
You were NEVER meant to win.
The game was a *"fixer"*.

But you were sold a LIE.
You were told you had a CHANCE.
You were told you could WIN.
If you worked HARD enough.
If you were TOUGH enough.
If you were SMART enough.
But that was all one big FUCKING lie.

So now you have a chance.
Now you can stop playing this INSANE game.
Make up your own rules.
Play your own game.
Why not give it a go?
You've got nothing to lose.
Except of course, your feeling of *"being FUCKED"*.
Don't die wondering what could have been.
Don't die without giving it a try.
Die with DIGNITY!
Die by saying *"At least I had a go!"*.
As *"Cranky Franky"* sang, *"I did it my way"*.

"The Don"
20.09.2020

Life & Death

(Vita e Morte)

It's one or the other.
One minute you're alive the next minute you're Dead.
One minute you walking the next minute you not.
One minute you're breathing the next minute you're not.
One minute you're alive the next minute you're Dead.

Life is like living on a knife's edge.
You never know when you're gonna be cut.
You never know when you're gonna fall.
It's a Life or Death situation.
There ain't no middle ground.
One minute you're alive & the next minute you're Dead.

It can happen at any time.
It can happen in any place.
Hopefully there'll be someone around.
Someone to help you into a safe place.
Because this journey we walk alone.
We can't do it with someone else.
All we can hope for is for someone to be around.
To help us when we are in this helpless state.

Life is such a fragile thing.
Life is such a delicate flower.
One minute it is so radiantly in bloom.
The next it is limp as dead fish.
One minute it is vibrant, pulsating & alive.
The next minute it is comatose, pale & lifeless.

You will never know when your time is up.
You will never know that your number has fallen.
There is no early calling card or txt message.
There are no red lights flashing that your end is near.
That your train has arrived at your final station.
That you've made your last journey.
That you will not be going home.

That you've eaten your last meal.
That you've drunk your last beer.
That you've had your last kiss.
Have you said your last goodbyes?
Probably not.
Because every moment could be your last.
This is Life & Death my friend.
It doesn't let you know when to say your last goodbyes.

"The Don"
20.09.2020

Message from an Alien
(Messaggio da un Alieno)

Earthlings!
What the fuck are you doing?
You are behaving like crazy people.
There is no my logic in your behaviour.
You acting like headless entities.
Your actions are chaotic.
Your actions are without purpose.
Your actions are destructive.
Your actions are irrational.
Your actions are incomprehensible.
Your actions are absurd.
Your actions make no sense.
Your actions are nonsense.
Your actions are destroying your planet.
Your actions are destroying yourselves.

We have been watching you from afar.
We have been seeing what you have been doing for quite a long time now.
We have been recording what you have been doing.
We are astonished at your actions.
For a self-defined "Intelligent species",
You have failed.
Please, do not classify yourselves as this.
This is for us to decide & to classify.
Our decision is, you are NOT!
We do NOT classify you as an "INTELLIGENT" species.
In fact, a species on your planet you call "Ants" are more Intelligent than you!
So please do not attempt to contact us.
We Will contact you.
When & if we're interested.
We are NOT interested.

Maybe we'll reassess your situation in a couple of thousand years.
Until then, "Good Luck".
You're gonna need it.
If you have any hope of surviving.
But we highly doubt it.
Unfortunately, we don't think you gonna survive the next hundred years.

"Message was received by SETI on 21st September 2020.
It was in all known Earth languages on the "International Mayday frequency, the Combined Distress and Emergency Frequency"
156.8 MHz: International Maritime Distress, Calling and Safety Frequency. 243.0 MHz: NATO".

"The Don"
21.09.2020

What is After Death?

(Cosa c'è Dopo la Morte)

Do not waste your time searching for this.
It is completely unnecessary.
It is a waste of your time.
It is a waste if your energy.
Instead you should be asking yourself,
"What is the meaning of life?"
"What is a meaningful life?"

This is more interesting.
This will ultimately be more beneficial to you.
This will bring you *"happiness"*.
This will bring you *"purpose"*.
This will bring you *"meaning"*.
This will bring you *"direction"*.

If you find an answer to this,
You will also get answer for all your other questions.
Because they are one & the same.
There is no Life if you are searching for the meaning of
Death.
But you are *"living"* Life if you are searching for Life.
The living is in the searching for its purpose.
Actually, *"Live Life"*.
Live *"Life"* to the *MAX*.
Don't waste it away.
Life is too precious to throw it away.
Live *"Life"* to the fullest, every moment of the day.
Live *"Life"* & you will find the meaning of *"Death"*.

"The Don"
21.09.2020

Desirable

(Auspicabile)

Do you think you are sexy?
Do you think you are beautiful?
Do you think you are wanted?
Do you think you are Desirable?

Do you have doubts about yourself!
Do you wonder if you've still got it?
Do you ask yourself if you're still fuckable?
Do you ask yourself if you're still Desirable?

Age creeps upon you whilst you are not looking.
It gets you in your sleep.
You wake up one morning,
And you see someone the mirror,
that you don't recognise!
And ask yourself "Am I still Desirable?"

Am I still beautiful?
Will anyone find me attractive?
Do I still have a HOT bod?
Would anyone want to sleep with me?
Would anyone want to fuck me?
Am I still Desirable?

I tell myself "It doesn't matter what others think about me".
I tell myself "The ONLY thing that the only thing that matters is what I
think about myself".
"Do I feel Beautiful?"
"Do I feel attractive?"
"Do I feel Sexy?"
"Do I feel wanted?"
"Do I feel fuckable?"
"Do I feel Desirable?"

If that is how you feel inside.
Then the answer is YES!
You are STILL Desirable!

"The Don"
22.09.2020

The Healing Game

(Il Gioco di Guarigione)

Let's play "The Healing Game".
It's easy to do.
You just have to be creative.
It doesn't matter in which way.
It doesn't matter how you do it.
You've just gotta let it all out.
All that shit that's inside you.
It's gonna have to come out.

It could be through writing.
It could be through poetry.
It could be through painting.
It could be through sculpture.
It could be through music.
It could be through dance.
It doesn't matter which it is.
But it's gotta be let out.

Life is part of a game.
Life is part of "The Healing Game".
You're born.
You're damaged.
You either stay damaged.
And you die damaged.
Or you play, "The Healing Game".
A game in which you have a chance to be healed.

The rules of the game are easy to learn.
The rules of the game are easy to follow.
All it requires is passion & commitment.
And you'll be playing like a true champion.
You'll see results straight away.
The scoreboard will be ticking over.

(Dedicated to Aurelie, my Romanian FB friend)

"The Don"

22.09.2020

Eileen, You See All the Wrong in the World
(Eileen, tu Vedi Tutto il Male del Mondo)

Eileen, you see all the wrong in the World.
And you want to fix it.
And you just get angry.
You wanna do something about it.
But you can't.
Just walk on by!
Let it go.
There's no need for you to react.

Eileen, you see all the wrong in the World.
And it makes you angry.
You wanna do something about it.
Even very small things.
They irritate you.
But don't "Sweat the small stuff!"
Walk on by.
Just let it go.
Accept that sometimes there is just nothing you can do.
And that's not a BAD thing.
That's just accepting REALITY.

Eileen, you see all the wrong in the World.
The tiniest infringement you see.
You have an "Eagle's Eye"
But you need to zoom out!
Look at the "Bigger Picture".
Take a couple of steps backwards.
Do not react.
Count to 10.
Clench your fist.
Bite your tongue.
Purse your lips.
Don't speak!

Eileen, you see all the wrong in the World.
And you want to fix it.

"The Don"
23.09.2020

Infatuation

(Infatuazione)

My *Infatuation* is over.
My *Longing* has stopped.
My *Desire* has disapated.
My *Passion* had quelled.
My *pain* has eased.
My *suffering* has subsided.
My *fantasies* have disappeared.
My *Mind* has quietened.
My *Broken He♥rt* has mended.
My *Lo♥e* has not stopped.

I think of you every now & then.
I don't think of you all the time.
I feel that I've broken the chain.

You no longer have power over my *He♥rt*.
You no longer have power over my *thoughts*.
You no longer have power over my *Lo♥e*.

I'm over my *infatuation*.

"The Don"
23.09.2020

L O  E

(Amore)

Lo💜e is such a misused word.
It is thrown around like confetti.
It's tossed out like loose change.
Everyone uses all the time!
They think they know what Lo💜e is.
But they are wrong.
They absolutely no idea about what Lo💜e is.

No one has really been taught what Lo💜e is.
No one has really experienced Lo💜e.
It's one big confusion.
It's one big mess.

Having sex is NOT Lo💜e.
Fucking is NOT Lo💜e.
Marriage is NOT Lo💜e.
Having children is NOT Lo💜e.
Being in a relationship is NOT Lo💜e.
Having a family is NOT Lo💜e.
Living together with someone is NOT Lo💜e.
Having material possessions is NOT Lo💜e.
Being beautiful is NOT Lo💜e.
Having lots of money is NOT Lo💜e.
Having POWER is NOT Lo💜e.
Being rich is not Lo💜e.
Being famous is NOT Lo💜e.
Saying that you Lo💜e someone is not Lo💜e.
Telling someone that you Lo💜e them is not Lo💜e.
Expecting Lo💜e is NOT Lo💜e.
Wanting Lo💜e is NOT Lo💜e.
Demanding Lo💜e is NOT Lo💜e.
Demanding to be Lo💜ed is NOT Lo💜e.

Lo💜e is an ACTION.
Lo💜e is verb.
Lo💜e is a doing thing.
Lo💜e is what YOU DO.
Lo💜e is how you behave.
Lo💜e is in your behaviour.
Lo💜e is in your actions.
Lo💜e is in how you treat other people.
Lo💜e is in how you treat other people ALL the time.
NOT just once or whenever you feel like it.

Love is a "State of Mind".
Love is in your Heart.
Love is in your Soul.
Love is on you very Being.
Love is Respect.
Love is Compassion.
Love is Friendship!

Love NEVER runs out.
Love lasts FOREVER.
Love is ETERNAL.
Love is the Universe.
Love is the Cosmos.

Love is YOU!

That's if you learn & understand what Love is.
And then put it into practice.
Love just doesn't happen by itself.
Love needs NURTURING.
Love needs to be tended to.
Love needs to be LIVED!

"The Don"
24.09.2020

They Tamed Maserati!

(Hanno Domato Maserati)

They tamed Porsche.
They tamed Chevrolet.
They tamed Mustang.
They tamed Austin Martin.
They tamed MG.
They tamed Corvette.
They tamed Lotus!
They tamed Jaguar.
They tamed Alfa Romeo.
They tamed Fiat.
They tamed Citroën.

I was sick in my stomach.
To see these wild things domesticated.
Turned into SUVs!
How could they?
How could we let this happen?
Now they are ALL the SAME!
Their individuality removed.
Their personality suffocated.
Their sexiness desexed!

Will they tame Ferrari?
Will they tame Lamborghini?

These are bland times indeed.
These are dark days.
These are boring years.
These are times without imagination.
These are times without magic.
These are times without creativity.

They even tamed Maserati!

"The Don"
24.09.2020

Bruised He♥rt
(Cuore Ammaccato)

I gave you my He♥rt.
But you only wounded it.
I didn't let you tear it apart.
That would have been disastrous.

My He♥rt is important to me.
My He♥rt is sacred.
My He♥rt is a vessel.
My He♥rt is a container.
My He♥rt is full of Lo♥e.

You can step on it.
You can throw it away.
You can tug at my He♥rt strings.
But you can NEVER break it.
It's too valuable.
It's too important.
It's too strong.

It can be hurt.
It can be sad.
It can be abused.
It can be refused.
It can be rejected.
It can be dejected.
It can be deflated.
It can be wounded.
It can be bruised.

But it CANNOT be BROKEN.
My He♥rt is STRONG!

"The Don"
25.09.2020

In the Company of Women
(In Compagnia delle Donne)

I Love women.
I Love the female body.
I Love the female mind.
I Love the female Heart.
I Love the female Soul.
I Love the beauty of a woman.
I Love the beauty of a naked woman's body.
I Love to touch their skin.
I Love to kiss the flesh.
I Love to run my hands over their naked form.
I Love to explore their curves.
I Love to dive into their hidden valleys.
I Love to cup their naked breasts.
I Love to kiss the nape of their necks.
I Love to run my tongue down their naked spine.
I Love to follow it to the ends of FOREVER.
I Love to explore their sacred cave.
I Love to stay & play at the entrance from which all life enters
this world.
I Love to play hide & seek inside this holy place.
I Love to stay a while.
I Love to experience of innocence.
I Love to feel the peace when in the womb.
I Love to recapture the Oneness of that before being born.

I Love to be in the company of woman.

"The Don"
25.09.2020

Original Thought

(Pensiero Originale)

"We stand on the shoulders of giants".
Einstein said that.
Can we ever have an "Original Thought"?
Can an idea truly ever be "Unique"?
Can an idea ever be truly "Original"?

Where do our ideas come from?
Can I "own" a thought?
Can I "own" an idea?
Can I ever say, "This idea is mine?"

Are we not just "sponges"?
Do we not just "absorb" what's around us?
Do we not just borrow from others around us?
Do we not just repurpose from what has come before?
Don't we just "beg, borrow & steal" from others?
Don't we just "appropriate"?

Nothing is "original".
Not really.
We just reshape things.
Rework & remodel them.
Maybe, add a new perspective.
Add a different "point of view".
This is the "best" we can.
But this is good enough for me.
Because the Only "original" thing is "Me".
My "Being".
My "Existence".
My thoughts are NOT!

"The Don"
25.09.2020

The Butterfly Effect

(L'effetto Farfalla)

There's a hurricane in China.
There's a cyclone in Fiji.
There's a tornado in Mississippi.
There's a tsunami in Japan.
There's a volcanic eruption in Indonesia.
There's a dust storm in Cairo.
There's a tidal wave in the Philippines.
There's a drought in New South Wales.
There's a plague of locusts in Wyoming.
There's a hurricane in Florida.
There's a famine in Ethiopia.
There's acid rain in China.
There's a "Hard Rain" in Russia.
There's an earthquake in New Zealand.
There are floods Australia.
There are wildfires in California.
There are fish falling from the sky in Jordon.
There's a butterfly flapping its wings in New Mexico.
There's a new born baby crying in Iran.
There's an old woman dying in Italy.
There's a caterpillar becoming a butterfly in Brazil.
There's a girl making Lo♥e for the very first time in
France.
There's a young virgin girl being exorcised in "The Eternal
City".
There's a Queen abdicating in England.
There's a young boy committing suicide in Germany.

"The Don"
26.09.2020

Ms Fucking Bitch

That's what she calls herself.
And I have to agree.
She IS a "FUCKING" bitch.
I know too well.
She lets me know it at every opportunity.
She puts me in my place quick smart.
She doesn't give you too much space to manoeuver about.

"The quick or the Dead",
I think is her motto.
Or maybe it could be,
"Don't take anyone alive".
Because that's how it is,
When you're playing with FIRE.

She seizes on any opportunity.
She doesn't mess about.
She'll put you in your place.
If you step out of line.

So, take your time.
Don't rush your actions.
Think out first.
Make a plan of attack.
Remember, there are NO second chances.
There's NO turning back.

Let her make the first moves
She likes to control.
Are you ready for the ride?
Many better men before you have tried.
Many have accepted the challenge.
All have FAILED.
Are you ready for the trip of your life time?
If not, step aside.

Let her take the lead.
She likes this position.
Wait for you turn.
Don't be too hasty.
Don't "over" react.
Let it unfold the way that it should.
Don't show you hand too early.
Do you know how to "bluff"?
Can you keep a straight face?
Are you ready for the long haul?
This is a long night you're in for.

The most important thing for you to do.
The simplest & yet the most difficult to carry through.

Is to be "patient".
Patience is the key here.
That's all you need to do.
Is wait for your turn.

You'll have to be clever though.
You'll have to pick up all the cues.
No misunderstanding.
No misinterpretation.
Be clear & precise.
Because she's ready to pounce.
At any indiscretion.
At any vague meanderings.

Are you well prepared?
Are you well versed?
Do you know about art?
Do you know about music?
Do you know about culture?
Do you know about politics?
Do you know about commerce?
Do you know about economics?
Do you know about travel?

You will need to be prepared in all these areas
And many, many more.
She knows it ALL.
She has lived it all in her 41 years on this planet.
She has lived many lives.
She lived in Las Vegas for a year when she was only 16.
And that's just the beginning of an "extra-ordinary" life.
So many stories she tells.
On our nights out on the balcony.
Getting drunk & stoned.
Listening to the most amazing array of musical genres.
From Blues, Jazz, folk, punk, world music to classic.
She knows it all.
She even remembers all the lyrics.
And sings along with them all.
In these moments of pure bliss & delight.
She seems to get transported to some way far off land.
I watch her face intently, keenly to see the expressions that see makes.
I become mesmerised & absorbed by them.
Watching every little twitch, every little movement.
I sit & I smile about nothing in particular.
Sometimes you don't need a reason to.
It's enough to just "Be".
And no explanation is needed.
"Oh Don! Give me a break!"

That's how I feel when I am with her.
She's a "Fucking " Bitch that's for sure.
But take it from me,
She is well worth it.

"The Don"
27.09.2020

Wishful Thinking

(Pensiero Speranzoso)

I wish it's her ringing.
I wish she'll call.
I wish she thinks about me
I wish she's thinking about me.
I wish wants me.
I wish she asks me out.
I wish she says yes.
I wish she'll wanna go.
I wish she'll say yes.
I wish so won't reject me.
I wish she wants me.
I wish she'll want me.
I wish she dreams about me.
I wish she daydreams about me.
I wish she'll sleep with me.
I wish she'll want to sleep with me.
I wish wants to fuck me.
I wish she's in Lo e with me.
I wish she LO ES me.
I wish this is not just wishful thinking.

"The Don"
28.09.2020

Intimacy

(Intimità)

What is *Intimacy*?
How do I know that I'm being *Intimate*?
Whom should I be *Intimate* with?
Can I be *Intimate* with anyone?

Can I share my deepest secrets with you?
Can I share my darkest thoughts with you?
Can I share my passions with you?
Can I share my desires with you?
Can I share my dreams with you?
Can I share my failures with you?
Can I share my rejections with you?
Can I share my fears with you?
Can I share my Lo♥e with you?
Can I share my He♥rt with you?
Can I share my Soul with you?
Can I share my Being with you?
Can I share my "Inner Child" with you?

Can I be "open" with you?
Can I be vulnerable with you?
Can I be submissive with you?
Can I be honest with you?
Can I be sensitive with you?
Can I be fragile with you?
Can I be innocent with you?
Can I be funny with you?
Can I be childish with you?
Can I be smart with you?
Can I be stupid with you?
Can I be INTIMATE with you?

"The Don"
28.09.2020

Friends Without Benefits

(Amici Senza Benefici)

I guess we're flatmates.
We are flatmates that sleep together.
We are the best of friends.
We are "friends without benefits".

We Lo♥e each other but we are not LO♥ERS.
We sleep together but we do not fuck.
We are best friends.
We are "friends without benefits".

We spoon each other.
We hug each other.
We hold each other.
We are "friends without benefits".

We don't kiss much anymore.
We hold hands sometimes.
We have a lot of laughs together.
I guess we are "friends without benefits".

We have been together for a very long time.
We'll probably be together forever.
We will be friends forever.
We are "friends without benefits".

"The Don"
30.09.2020

How Can We Sleep While Our Earth is Burning?
(Come Possiamo Dormire Mentre la Nostra Terra Brucia?)

Hottest year on record.
Mega bushfires in Australia.
Complete towns destroyed.
Hundreds killed.
Thousands of animals killed.
Koalas almost extinct.

Weather patterns changing.
Weather patterns becoming unpredictable.
More extreme weather predicted.
More fires.
More floods.
More droughts.
More hotter days.
More cyclones.
More hurricanes.

Mega wildfires in California.
Ocean temperature rising faster than anticipated.
Coral reefs in the Great Barrier Reef are dying.
Ice shelves in the Antarctic are melting.
Permafrost in Siberia is melting.
Glaciers in Iceland are melting.
Thousands of fish found dead.
The most devastating hurricanes & cycles in recorded history.
The most destructive tornadoes on record.
Torrential flooding India.
Heatwave conditions throughout Europe.
Severest drought in Australia EVER.
Hundreds of Pilot Whales commit suicide in Tasmania.
Extinction of animal species at a rate NEVER seen before.

Politicians not listening.
Politicians not seeing.
Politicians not acting.
Politicians deny "Climate Change" is responsible.
They claim it is poor or no bush management.

Greta Thumberg where are you?
Thank God for Sir Richard Attenborough.
How can we sleep while our Earth is burning?

"Ah, this world is burning fast
Oh, this world will never last
I don't want to lost it here in my time
Give me time forever here in my time."

"O Caritas" from "Catch Bull at Four" by Cat Stevens, 1972

"The Don"
01.10.2020

Don't Sweat the Small Stuff

(Non Sudare le Piccole Cose)

Be cool.
Be chilled.
Be relaxed.
Be calm.
Be easy.

Don't panic.
Don't stress.
Don't freak out.
Don't lose your head.
Don't lose your cool.

Keep it together.
Keep it under control.
Keep it in check.
Keep it balanced.

Look at the big picture.
Look at the bigger picture.
Look at it from another point of view.
Look at it from all angles.
Look at it with new eyes.

Take a deep breath.
Take a couple of steps backwards.
Take your time.
Take time to collect your thoughts.

Say to yourself:
"It's ALL good!"
"Everything will work in the End!"
"And if it hasn't worked out,
It's NOT the End!"

"The Don"
02.10.2020

Heroes

(Eroi)

We are all heroes.
We are all heroes every day.
We are all heroes every fucking day.
We are all heroes not matter what you say.
We are all heroes no matter what they fucking say.
We are all heroes no matter what they do.
We are all heroes no matter what they fucking do.
We are all heroes in spite of them.
We are all heroes everyday & every night.
We are all heroes through it all.
We are all heroes through thick & thin.

We are all heroes because we keep on struggling.
We are all heroes because we keep on fighting.
We are all heroes because we never give in.
We are all heroes because we never give up.
We are all heroes because we are right
We are all heroes because we have to survive.
We are all heroes because we dare to Hope.
We are all heroes because we have Dignity.
We are all heroes because we have Integrity.
We are all heroes because we have Passion.
We are all heroes because we have Soul.
We are all heroes because we have a He♥rt.
We are all heroes because we LO♥E.

We are all *HEROES!*
We are all *HEROES!*
We are all *HEROES!*
We are all *HEROES!*

HEROES!
HEROES!
HEROES!
HEROES!

"The Don"
03.10.2020

It's All Good

(Va Tutto Bene)

It's all fine.
Nothing to worry about.
Ease your troubled mind.
Let it all roll.
Just relax.
Don't panic.
Be cool.
What are you worrying about?
The World won't end.
It's not the end of The World.
The Sun will rise tomorrow.
Tomorrow is another day.
Live in The Moment.
Worrying won't change anything.
What will be, will be.
Be positive.
Look on the bright side of Life.
Walk on the sunny side of the road.
See the glass as half full.
Be optimistic.
See the funny side of things.
Look at the funny side of Life.
Laugh at your problems.
Laugh at yourself.
Laugh at Life.
See the humour in things.
See the beauty all around you.
See the nice things in people.
Don't complain.
Don't whinge!
And try to remember,
It's ALL good!

"The Don"
03.10.2020

Vacuum

(Vuoto)

Do not respond.
Do not act.
Do not stop.
Do not communicate.
Leave empty space.
Create a "Black Hole".
Don't think.

Empty your Head.
Empty your Mind.
Empty your thoughts.
Empty your He♥rt.
Empty your Lo♥e.

Keep living.
Keep moving on
Keep going forward
Keep doing.
Keep looking forward.
Keep being alive.

Become detached.
Become disconnected
Become dispossessed.
Become disentangled.
Become removed.
Become distant.
Become strong.

Create a vacuum.

"The Don"
04.10.2020

Hurting

(Ferito)

I went to save her.
But I was the one that needed saving.
I went to look out for her.
But I was the one needing looked after.
I went to find her,
But I was the one that lost.
I went to search for her,
But I be was the one that was needing to be found.
I went to search for Lo♥e her,
But I be was the one that was needing to be Lo♥ed.
I went to help for her,
But I be was the one that was needing to be helped.
I went to protect for her,
But I be was the one that was needing to be protected.
I went to untrap for her,
But I be was the one that was needing to be untrapped.
I went to unchain for her,
But I be was the one that was needing to be unchained.
I went to search for her,
But I be was the one that was needing to be found.

I was the one that was lonely.
I was the one that was shattered.
I was the one that was broken.
I was the one that was damaged.
I was the one that was crying.
I was the one that was Dying.

"The Don"
04.10.2020

I Can't Be Your Friend

(Non Posso Essere Tuo Amico)

I enjoy the time we spend together.
The nights full of songs,
Full of singing,
Full of dancing,
Full of drinking,
Full of smoking dope.
Full of getting "stoned",
Full of deep conversations,
Full of laughter,
Full of unrequited Lo♥e.

But I can't be your friend,
I suffer too much.
If only I was stronger.
Maybe, it could be then.
But I am weak.
I give in to my desires.
I know it sounds pathetic.
I think it's "the best" for me.
For my own sanity.
Sorry, but I can't be your friend.

"The Don"
05.10.2020

I Still Have a Lot of Work to Do

(Ho Ancora Molto Lavoro da Fare)

I'm a *"Work in Progress"*.
I'm a work incomplete.
I'm an unfinished masterpiece.
I still have a lot of work to do.

I thought I was finished.
I thought I had it under control.
I thought I was on *"top of it"*.
I still have a lot of work to do.

When it came to the *"test"*.
When it came to put it into action.
When I had to put *"my feet where my mouth was"*.
I still have a lot of work to do.

I FAILED.
I *"collapsed on my own sword"*.
I ran like a *"coward"*.
I still have a lot of work to do.

I *"Freaked Out"*.
I lost my bravado.
I lost my confidence.
I still have a lot of work to do.

I saw my competition.
I saw my opponent.
I saw my fears.
I still have a lot of work to do.

He was standing there like a cat that had just swallow a fat rat.
He was leaning there like a victorious gladiator.
She was nestled close to him like a prize he had just won.
I realise then that, I still have a lot of work to do.

I was the vanquished one.
I was the loser.
I was the beaten, bloodied & bruised, *"nobody"*.
It was then that I knew, I still Have a lot of work to do.

I felt paralysed.
I felt an emptiness inside.
I felt reality hit me in the face.
It was then that I knew, I still have a lot of work to do.

In that moment I lost all hope.
In that moment I felt rejection.
In that moment I felt destroyed.
It was then that I knew, I still have a lot of work to do.

Every experience is a learning one.
And this one was that for me.
It was a good *"slap in the face"* for me.
Because I realised that, I still have a lot of work to do.

"The Don"
05.10.2020

It Never Existed

(Non è Mai Esistito)

It was all illusory.
It was a delusion.
It was all in my Mind.
It NEVER existed.
How can something be over if it never existed?

It was all in my Head.
It was all *"make believe"*.
It was all a fantasy.
It NEVER existed.
How can something be over if it never existed?

I wanted it to exist.
I wanted it to be real.
I wanted it be something that it wasn't.
It NEVER existed.
How can something be over if it never existed?

It was all wishful thinking.
It was all hopeful thoughts.
It was all one big *"daydream"*.
However, it NEVER existed.
How can something be over if it never existed?

I wanted it to be something more.
I wanted her to Lo♥e me.
I wanted her to feel my Lo♥e.
But it NEVER existed.
How can something be over if it never existed?

I wanted her to want me.
I wanted her to Desire me.
I want her to wanna fuck me.
But it NEVER existed.
How can something be over if it never existed?

It was all crazy wishes on my part.
It was all just silly desire.
It was one big construction in my head.
Because it NEVER existed.
How can something be over if it never existed?

There is nothing to get *"over"*.
There is nothing to be sad about.
There is nothing to cry over.
Because it NEVER existed.
How can something be over if it never existed?

It NEVER existed.
Realise this fact.

It NEVER existed.
It was just in my Head.

It NEVER existed.
It cannot be Dead.

It NEVER existed.
And that is that.

It NEVER existed.
And that is a fact.

It NEVER existed.
No point looking back.

It NEVER existed.
There are no *"maybes"* or *"what ifs"*.

It NEVER existed.
It is what it is.

It NEVER existed.
Let it go & move on.

It NEVER existed.
Expunge it from my mind.

It NEVER existed.
Expel it from my thoughts.

It NEVER existed.
I've gotta stop think about it.

It NEVER existed.
That's the TRUTH & there is no denying it.

It NEVER existed.
I believe that.

It NEVER existed.
Say that to myself.

It NEVER existed.
Say it over & over again.

It NEVER existed.
It NEVER existed.
It NEVER existed.
It NEVER existed.

"The Don"
05.10.2020

Books written by "The Don"

"My Life with Chickens & other stories: I Pity the Poor Immigrant"
Published:
10th September, 2019
Autobiography Book 1: 0 – 12 years old

"Poems for Misfits, Miscreants, Misanthropes, Mavericks, Losers & Malcontents!"
Published:
10th June, 2020
Book of Poems 1

"Poems for Troubled Minds & Trouble Hearts"
Published:
10th August, 2020
Book of Poems 2

"My Life in a CULT & other stories: Everybody Must Get STONED!"
Published:
10th September, 2020
Autobiography Book 2: 15 – 30 years old

"Poems for Restless Minds & Restless Hearts"
Published:
10th October, 2020
Book of Poems 3

"Poems for Anarchists, Revolutionaries, Outlaws & Dissidents!"
Published:
10th November, 2020
Book of Poems 4

"Poems for Non-Thinkers & Eccentrics"
Published:
10th December, 2020
Book of Poems 5

"The Rantings of a Madman"
Published:
10th January, 2021
Book of Poems 6

"Poems for Desperate Lovers & Silent Voices"
Published:
10th February, 2021
Book of Poems 7

"Poems for Tormented Minds & Tortured Souls"
Published:
10th March, 2021
Book of Poems 8

All available ONLY online